HARDENING ROCK

hardening rock

an organic anthology of the adolescence of rock 'n roll

edited and with an introduction
by bruce l. chipman

with an appreciative essay by x. j. kennedy

little, brown and company · boston · toronto

Published simultaneously in Canada by Little, Brown & Company (Canada) Limited

Printed in the United States of America

This is for Pamela, my family, the three DB's, Gordon, and, parenthetically, Mr. Quickly, with love.

acknowledgments

Many thanks are due Bill Phillips, one of Little, Brown's finest, and X J Kennedy for their tireless guidance. And Pam too. For their enthusiasm, I thank Gordon Salisbury and Dick McDonough; for valued research services, thanks to the Index Departments of BMI and ASCAP. Finally, for assistance in typing, thanks to Phyll Habib.

CONTENTS

iNTRODUCTiON

Ladies and gentlemen, I'd like to do a song now that tells a little story, that really makes a lot of sense —

Awopbopaloobop — alopbamboom!
Tutti-frutti! All rootie!
Tutti-frutti! All rootie!

— Elvis Presley, 1956

What I'm trying to defend is my right and your right to go to a church of our choice, or buy the record of our choice.

— Dick Clark

This retrospective glance at the adolescence of American rock 'n roll was spurred by the love and intimate kinship I feel for nearly all "dusty diamonds" (or, if you will, "mossy bossies," "moldy golden oldies," "hits from the grooveyard," ad nauseam). We do not react aesthetically to these songs nor can we pretend their straightforward lyrics to be literate or poetic; rather, it is the personal — and sometimes very emotional — remembrance of things past evoked by the records that has determined their value for us. Rock 'n roll has, in a sense, "created" those of us who grew up with it: we have become what we listened to and bopped to. When our parents knocked the rock, they knocked our very identities. As one observer, Ralph J. Gleason, noted, "all of a sudden the *New Yorker* joke about the married couple dreamily remarking, when a disc jockey played 'Hound Dog' by Elvis, 'they're playing our song,' wasn't a joke any longer. It was real. That generation had suddenly grown up and married and Elvis was real memories of real romance and not just kid stuff."

This idiosyncratic sampling includes a broad cross-section of lyrics from the Golden Age of rock 'n roll, 1954 through 1963. This formative decade began with the "rockabilly" rhythm and blues of Bill Haley and the Comets of "Rock Around the Clock" fame. Said Haley of those early times (as quoted in Charlie Gillett's *The Sound of the City*): "Around the early fifties the musical world was starved for something new . . . the days of the solo vocalist and the big bands had gone . . . I felt then that if I could take, say, a Dixieland tune and drop the first and third beats, and accentuate the second and the fourth, and add a beat the listeners could clap to as well as dance to this would be what they were after."

And it turned out to be a winning formula—remember Record Review on Dick Clark's *American Bandstand* and how any successful platter *had* to be danceable? After Haley, the pop charts reflected a shift to three black rockers: Little Richard, Fats Domino, and, perhaps most important, Chuck Berry. The songs of Berry are heavily emphasized in this collection, for he is, as Richard Goldstein says in *The Poetry of Rock*, "America's first rock poet . . . He virtually defined rock for the generation to come as the sound of an inner volcano, the hum of satisfied machinery . . . [Berry] produced an authentic rock libretto of America in the fifties." Cool, snazzy, and subtly coy, he was *the* mythmaker for millions of hepcats and dungaree dolls. Chuck Berry, above all others, managed to capture almost every nuance of fifties teen life.

Progressing through orgasmic Elvis and the likes of the Everly Brothers, rock 'n roll reached its commercial crest when it became citified, both via the urban groups and Top 40 radio (called by Paul Williams in *Outlaw Blues* "the birthplace and childhood home of rock music"). This decade of adolescence ended with the invasion of the Beatles and the Stones and with the introduction of sophisticated electronic recording techniques. The ten years of innocence that had begun with "It's Howdy Doody Time!" ended abruptly with an assassination—and we were somehow no longer kids or even teen-agers anymore. We were forced to awaken from our "teendream" and spit out our bubblegum; the special moments of innocence as reflected in our songs were driven out of our young lives by the "relevant" sixties. It was a much more serious change than the one from bobby-sox to stockings, for the world now demanded substance of our images. Because we were forced to do some fast growing, those "Shake, Rattle and Roll" times lost to us became all the more valuable.

PEANUT GALLERY

Music had been the byword of our adolescent culture, a culture formed around the first youth movement of freedom in America. Rock 'n roll belonged *solely* to teen-agers and was directed exclusively toward our sympathies—it was an infant the adult world wanted no part of. The styles of the singers and the images engendered by their songs were cultural forces: molding tastes and making us aware of mores we didn't know we had. The lyrics collected here all enjoyed national play, but they weren't necessarily the most popular—if indeed sales figures matter much to the individual seeker after nostalgia, who will, I suspect, have his own special song at the top of his personal chart. This book directs itself especially to two audiences: to those of us twenty-five to thirty-five years old who have experienced these songs firsthand and have installed more than a few as permanent fixtures in our heads, and to the teen-agers of today who are examining the roots of their own music.

The fifties and early sixties, years of mass muscle-flex for the young, is that otherwise inauspicious slot in this century which saw the discovery/invention of teen-agerism. Prior to the early fifties, an American youth culture was nonexistent; however, as movies, television, and radio tentacled out and as the spending power of young people asserted itself, there developed a solid concept of American teen which before had been only regional in scope. A tribal unity of transistor sisters and brothers was created through the communal message of teen beat—as a cultural force, our music defined, reflected, and created images of teenhood. And with this music emerged a profound sense of the new sector of Americans "'twixt twelve and twenty," as Pat Boone tagged us, with vast resources of untapped commercial potential. We children of the fifties discovered ourselves largely through rock 'n roll, and it is not surprising that the image makers themselves caught upon *that* music in order to package and reproduce us for ourselves. (As a model we were offered Fabian, the successfully processed and plasticized rock 'n roll star.) This new kind of music was treated as a commodity, no more than a product by adults; for us, however, it was a major form of communication, something to be taken seriously, an art strictly for us. As the youth culture solidified its purchasing power through mammoth record sales, manufacturers sought both to supply the goods we "had to have" (records, fan mags, etc.) and to create demands within teendom to promote growth and diversity (sheet music, guitars, radios). Remember how *All-American Boy* urged each of us to buy a guitar so that every kid could become a rock 'n roll singer who drove a big car and the girls mad. We were weaned on the concept that material goods were the criteria of success, of "cool." Ironically, the new *free* entertainment provided by television, whose primary message was commercial, led us to become one of America's prime purchasing groups. A great deal of our time was spent finding out what was "in" this week; the remainder of the time and all our dough was taken up buying the latest record, getting flattops with fenders or Toni home permanents, and learning the right lingo—we all had to *belong*.

But this time of imitation and emulation spawned a kind of group pride, a sense of identity to be shared only by teen-agers. And it was rock 'n roll that had nourished and consoled us at times when our parents just didn't seem to understand what it was all about. Our music spoke to us directly and reminded us that we were not alone in our feelings.

Bruce L. Chipman

HARDENING ROCK

Back in those pre-Presley early 1950s when rock 'n roll was gestating, pop music was spoiling for a change. In return for your dime, a jukebox would ladle out a small package of sentiment (sold for the prevention of reality only): maybe Perry Como singing "Wanted," or Tony Bennett's "Because of You," Jo Stafford's "You Belong to Me," Eddie Fisher's "Oh My Papa"; maybe Little Jimmy Boyd's "I Saw Mommy Kissing Santa Claus" or the song from *Moulin Rouge* or (after Truman fired General MacArthur in 1951) "Old Soldiers Never Die, They Just Fade Away." Not that all of these songs were execrable, you understand; but after rock 'n roll got done with them, they seemed like a gallon of near beer chased with a shot of mountain lightning.

An adolescent in the previous decade of World War Two, I recall wondering even then: what in heck were these jukeboxes moaning about, anyhow? About just kissing — or about doing the big number itself? At least, when rock and roll arrived, you didn't have to wonder. Oafish, unreal, jejune, and sentimental as many of their lyrics still were, rock songs had at least one major difference: their driving beat. A rock singer might bewail his mistress's love in words as pure as Jack Frost sugar, but all the while that steady slam of his powerful guitar told you that (musically, anyway) something was going on below the belt. The guitar, formerly an inaudible prop that a big band's male vocalist used to fool around with so he wouldn't look silly just sitting there, now amplified, became the central pulse. If any doubt remained in anybody's mind that rock 'n roll was about mere kissing, then Elvis Presley, with cobra hips, must have punctured it with his very first thrust. One sexual wail from his pipes and every nice girl in the nation must have felt like throwing away her UNICEF collection box and hopping on the east end of a motorcycle gunning west.

And the nice thing about it was that she could feel that way without actually taking any risks. No rock singer ever seduced an audience — not onstage, that is; although there are histories of teeny-boppers who, in Bacchantean frenzy at rock concerts, ripped up their theatre seats and tried to violate themselves with the fragments. Elders might scowl, and did; but it was mostly just good clean sublimation. There was, however, an appreciable rise in the birth rate within a year after Bill Haley and the Comets burst upon the national scene in 1955 with "Rock Around the Clock," and there's no doubt some truth in the words to "Who Put the Bomp in the Bomp Ba Bomp Ba Bomp":

> *I'd like to thank the guy who wrote the song*
> *That made my baby fall in love with me.*

Rock concerts, I suspect, must have produced a few modern "camp-meeting babies" (as Americans a century earlier used to call those by-products of the emotion-wringing sermons of evangelists).

On the whole, though, Bruce Chipman's selection of golden oldies will probably stir much more innocent memories. Looking back on these lyrics now, what strikes you is the way in which, in most of them, the values of their society are taken for granted. Be true to your school, one message runs. Go to chapel, be baptized, married, and interred, with Little Jimmy Brown. Far from ready to bare her charms in front of a throng at Woodstock, their typical teeny-bopper shrivels with maidenly reticence when she first wears her itsy bitsy teenie weenie yellow polkadot bikini. She accepts love only "as long as God has no objections," and ends up wedded to the boy who always buys on the installment plan. "Gather ye rosebuds" seems to be the moral — whiz around, kids, in that little deuce coupe, but face up to the fact that in the end you'll get a job (sha da da da da), make yourself live with blue monday, and finally end on the great American used-car lot of old age (if you're not lucky enough to die in a drag race first).

In their public lives, most popular rock idols of the day confirmed this. No audience-assaulting Zappas back then ("Hello, pigs!"), no propriety-smashing Jim Morrisons. Back in that innocent age, the stars came on as surprisingly conventional niceguys: seventeen-year-old Phil Spector naming his first hit tune by lifting a line from his father's gravestone ("To Know Him Is to Love Him"). Little Richard temporarily stopping out at the peak of his career to serve time in a seminary. Elvis the model soldier faithfully serving his Uncle Sam and loyally buying his aging mother a pink Cadillac.

But here and there you catch in these songs the stirring of discontent, or at least of a little passive resistance. It's a bitter view, in "Don't Wake Up the Kids," of the hypocritical parents who pitch a big booze party to impress friends, robbing the kids' pigbanks and ending hungover. Protest, of a sort, informs these hot-rod and drag-race ballads: "Dead Man's Curve," "Shut Down," "Drag City." Evidently, one way to get the hell out of adult society is to tromp down hard on the gas. A few heroes of these songs tromp so hard they escape permanently. Among the seven songs in the section called "Tragedy," you can count one death by plane crash, three deaths by drowning, and three by car accidents. Such melodramatic self-immolation really peaks in the song "Teen Angel," in which one lover, retrieving the other lover's high school ring, is creamed by an onrushing train. And then there's the Gothic claptrap horror of "Who Do You Love?"—maybe designed to show the singer as a ghoul whom not even a mother ought to love. It was probably no coincidence that some of the best-selling comic books of the period were Vault of Horror and Tales from the Crypt, in which fourteen-year-old torturers used to have wild times carving up various authority figures, usually senile. And what significance, if any, was there in those mass stampedes to the drive-ins to watch I Was a Teen-age Werewolf and I Was a Teen-age Frankenstein (both 1957)? To imagine oneself transformed into a monster, fangs and all, may have been one way to strike back against adult tyranny. In such a climate of reverie, an occasional song of chill realism like "Blue Monday" or "Money Honey" breaks like a bucket of icewater.

In those primitive days—when being busted meant needing a dollar, when having a bad trip meant an airline's losing your luggage, when getting stoned meant drinking too many beers—who could have guessed the future? Still to come was that psychedelic institution and acid-rock-and-light show. Ahead lay the song that couldn't possibly be staged but only studioed, and the Beatles' 1964 sweep of America. There would be Dylan's "The Times

They Are A-Changing"; new faces (Hendrix, Joplin, Mama Cass); new groups (Rolling Stones, Jefferson Airplane, the Mothers, the Doors, Cream, Who). Not just in the greater complexity of their lyrics and their melodies but in the problems they'd share with their auditors, some of these later productions make those of 1954–1963 look very clean and gangling, and not a little wet behind the ears.

It's lucky that none of us is as old as the quantity of change he's seen. If that were the method of reckoning, then anyone aged seventeen in 1950 might now be a grayhair of seventy. H-bombs, moon landings, coast-to-coast color TV, new war, new peace talks, Red China in the UN—all of which ought to give anybody now above thirty the right to pause, recall "Heartbreak Hotel," feel in his pelvic muscles a sympathetic twinge, and even, perhaps, look back with a certain wistfulness.

X. J. Kennedy

Teen-age Heaven

I dreamed I was in teen-age heaven,
I saw all the stars in teen-age heaven.
There was a golden door
With a golden star;
And I walked on through
And there were all the teen-age stars we knew-oo-oo:
There was Richie Valens singing "Donna, I love you";
Next to him was Buddy Holly singing "Yuk yuk, Peggy Sue";
Eddie Cochran sang "Summertime Blues" into a golden mike;
The Big Bopper, with his laughing face, said, "You know what I like."
On the movie scene I saw James Dean, well, what can I say?
Then an angel led me to the room marked A HUNDRED YEARS FROM TODAY.
There was Ricky Nelson singing "Lonesome Town,"
And all the stars then gathered 'round:
Bobby Vee, Brenda Lee, and Fabian too,
Connie Francis, Neil Sedaka, the Fleetwoods sang "Mr. Blue."
And there was Elvis in a suit of gold singing at his very best
"Don't Be Cruel," "Love Me Tender"—you know all the rest.
And as I left teen-age heaven Duane played his guitar;
Then I heard them call the roll, and the names were teen-age stars.

GROWING PAINS AND TEEN TRAUMA

Sweet Little Sixteen

They're really rockin' in Boston, in Pittsburgh, P.A.,
Deep in the heart of Texas, and 'round the Frisco Bay.
All over St. Louis, 'way down in New Orleans,
All the cats wanna dance with sweet little sixteen.

Sweet little sixteen, she's just got to have
About a half a million famed autographs.
Her wallet's filled with pictures, she gets 'em one by one;
Becomes so excited, watch her, look at her run

They're really rockin' in Boston, in Pittsburgh, P.A.,
Deep in the heart of Texas, and 'round the Frisco Bay.
All over St. Louis, 'way down in New Orleans,
All the cats wanna dance with sweet little sixteen.

Sweet little sixteen, she's got the grown-up blues,
Tight dresses and lipstick, she's sportin' high-heel shoes.
Oh, but tomorrow morning, she'll have to change her trend
And be sweet sixteen and back in class again.

> Oh, Mommy, Mommy,
> Please may I go?
> It's such a sight to see
> Somebody steal the show.
> Oh, Daddy, Daddy,
> I beg of you,
> Whisper to Mommy,
> It's all right with you.

'Cause they'll be rockin' on Bandstand in Philadelphia, P.A.,
Deep in the heart of Texas, and 'round the Frisco Bay.
All over St. Louis, 'way down in New Orleans,
All the cats wanna dance with sweet little sixteen.

Itsy Bitsy Teenie Weenie Yellow Polkadot Bikini

She was afraid to come out of the locker,
She was as nervous as she could be;
She was afraid to come out of the locker,
She was afraid that somebody would see.

(Two, three, four — Tell the people what she wore.)
It was an itsy bitsy teenie weenie yellow polkadot bikini
That she wore for the first time today.
An itsy bitsy teenie weenie yellow polkadot bikini,
So in the locker she wanted to stay.
(Two, three, four — stick around, we'll tell you more.)

She was afraid to come out in the open,
And so a blanket around her she wore;
She was afraid to come out in the open,
And so she sat bundled up on the shore.

(Two, three, four — tell the people what she wore.)
It was an itsy bitsy teenie weenie yellow polkadot bikini,
That she wore for the first time today.
An itsy bitsy teenie weenie yellow polkadot bikini,
So in the blanket she wanted to stay.
(Two, three four — stick around, we'll tell you more.)

Now she's afraid to come out of the water,
And I wonder what she's gonna do;
Now she's afraid to come out of the water,
And the poor little girl's turning blue.

(Two, three, four — tell the people what she wore.)
It was an itsy bitsy teenie weenie yellow polkadot bikini,
That she wore for the first time today.
An itsy bitsy teenie weenie yellow polkadot bikini,
So in the water she wanted to stay.

 From the locker to the blanket,
 From the blanket to the shore;
 From the shore to the water,
 Guess there isn't any more.

12

Shop Around

When I became of age,
My mother called me to her side.
She said, "Son, you're growing up now;
Pretty soon you'll take a bride."

And then she said, "Just because you've become a young man now,
There's still some things that you don't understand now.
Before you ask some girl for her hand now,
Keep your freedom for as long as you can now."
My mama told me, "You'd better shop around."
Woh, yeah, you'd better shop around.
"Ah, hah, there's some things that I want you to know now.
Just as sure as the wind's gonna blow now,
The women come and the women gonna go now.
Before you tell 'em that you love 'em so now."
My mama told me, "You'd better shop around."
Woh, yeah, you'd better shop around.

"Try to find yourself a bargain, son.
Don't be sold on the very first one.
Pretty girls come a dime a dozen.
Try to find one who's gonna give you true loving.
Before you take a girl and say 'I do' now,
Make sure she's in love with you now,
Make sure that her love is true now.
I hate to see you feeling sad and blue now."
My mama told me, "You'd better shop around."

14

Peek-a-Boo

When you come home from the dance,
Stand in the hall and make a romance,
When you do the things you shouldn't do—
Peek-a-boo! I'm watchin' you.

When you ought to be in school,
Learning about the golden rule,
When you tell a tale that isn't true—
Peek-a-boo! I'm watchin' you.

> Look in the dark—you'll see my face;
> Don't try to hide—I'm ev'ry place.
> Play it cool, kind and sweet;
> I'm gonna give you hot feet!

Hope you heard the things I said;
Let it sink in your big hard head.
When you dance the sole right off your shoes—
Peek-a-boo! I'm watchin' you.

Don't Wake Up the Kids

Ma and Pa, now here you go again
Giving a party, trying to impress a friend.
We've been trying to figure what you spent;
This party must have cost a pretty cent. Hollerin'

Rack 'em back, let 'em stack, run 'em around again.
Rack 'em back, let 'em stack, run 'em around again.
Sh! Don't wake up the kids, don't wake up the kids.

Look at 'em do that old-time jitterbug,
Tearin' it up, the brand-new living room rug.
And when you find a hole burned in the chair,
You'll swear with all your might we put it there. Hollerin'

Rack 'em back, let 'em stack, run 'em around again.
Rack 'em back, let 'em stack, run 'em around again.
Sh! Don't wake up the kids, don't wake up the kids.

They say that there's a recession goin' on;
Whatcha gonna do when all your loot is gone?
You call all four of us a bunch of cranks
When we don't let you rob our piggy banks. Hollerin'

Rack 'em back, let 'em stack, run 'em around again.
Rack 'em back, let 'em stack, run 'em around again.
Sh! Don't wake up the kids, don't wake up the kids.

While all the kids were peeping through the cracks,
The baby found the kitchen in the back.
From the way he looks we've got a hunch
He musta got a hold of some of your punch. Hollerin'

Rack 'em back, let 'em stack, run 'em around again.
Rack 'em back, let 'em stack, run 'em around again.
Sh! Don't wake up the kids, don't wake up the kids.

Get up, you brats, and all of you grab a broom,
Follow me to that dirty living room.
And don't you make no noise while you sweep;
You know your father's ill and he's trying to sleep. Hollerin'

Rack 'em back, let 'em stack, run 'em around again.
Rack 'em back, let 'em stack, run 'em around again.
Sh! Don't wake up the kids, don't wake up the kids.

Almost Grown

Yeah, I'm doing all right in school,
They ain't said I've broke no rule,
I ain't never been in Dutch,
I don't browse around too much.

Don't bother me, leave me alone,
Anyway I'm almost grown.

I don't run around with no mob,
I got myself a little job,
I'm gonna buy myself a little car,
I'll drive my girl in the park.

Don't bother me, leave me alone,
Anyway I'm almost grown.

I got my eye on a little girl,
Ah, she's really out of this world,
When I take her out to a dance,
She's gotta talk about romance.

Don't bother us, leave us alone,
Anyway we're almost grown.

You know I'm still livin' in town,
But done married and settled down.
Now I really have a ball,
So I don't browse around at all.

Don't bother us, leave us alone,
Anyway we're almost grown.

Teen-ager's Prayer

What is a teen-ager's prayer?
That's not very hard to define;
All they want out of life
Is love and peace of the mind.

I will explain it to you,
Just what it's all about:
It is something that's really big
Both day and night.

On bended knees they'll beg and plead
For a love that is true.
Won't you give them love, just a little bit of love?
'Cause you see that's the least anybody can do.

Here is a teen-ager's prayer:
I know you care;
Won't you give them their share
Of the teen-ager's prayer?

He's Sure the Boy I Love

I always dreamed the boy I loved would come along
And he'd be tall and handsome, rich and strong.
Now that boy I love has come to me,
But he sure ain't the way I thought he'd be.

He doesn't look like a movie star,
He doesn't drive a Cadillac car.
He sure ain't the boy I've been dreamin' of,
But he's sure the boy I love.

Let me tell ya now, he'll never be a big businessman,
He always buys on the installment plan.
He sure ain't the boy I've been dreamin' of,
But he's sure the boy I love.

When he holds me tight,
Ev'rything's right,
Crazy as it seems.
I'm his,
Whatever he is,
And I forget all of my dreams.

And ev'rybody knows that he doesn't hang diamonds 'round my neck
And all he's got's an unemployment check.
He sure ain't the boy I've been dreamin' of,
But he's sure the boy I love.

James (Hold the Ladder Steady)

James and I — we went to Mama
And showed her my diamond ring.
She said, "My poor little baby, you must be crazy
To think of such a thing."

So! James, James,
Hold the ladder steady;
James, James,
I'm packed and I am ready.
James, James,
Hold the ladder steady;
I'm a-comin' down to your arms.
I'm a-comin' down to your arms.

James and I — we went to Daddy
And said, "Dad, we want to be wed."
Dad said, "Nope, you'll just have to elope!"
And laughed as he went to bed.

So! James, James,
Hold the ladder steady,
James, James,
I'm packed and I am ready.
James, James,
Hold the ladder steady;
I'm a-comin' down to your arms.
I'm a-comin' down to your arms.

I'd hate to see 'em in the morning when
They both completely flip!
He'll be saying, "They can't!"
She'll be feelin' faint,
And I'll be kissin' my husband's lips!

So! James, James,
Hold the ladder steady;
James, James,
I'm packed and I am ready.
James, James,
Hold the ladder steady;
I'm a-comin' down to your arms.
I'm a-comin' down to your arms.

You Never Can Tell

It was a teen-age wedding and the old folks wished 'em well,
You could see that Pierre did truly love the mademoiselle.
And now the young monsieur and madame have rung the chapel bell.
"C'est la vie," say the old folks; it goes to show you never can tell.

They furnished off an apartment with a two-room Roebuck sale,
The coolerator was crammed with TV dinners and ginger ale.
But when Pierre found work, the little money comin' worked out well.
"C'est la vie," say the old folks; it goes to show you never can tell.

They had a hi fi phono; boy, did they let it blast,
Seven hundred little records all rockin' rhythm and jazz.
But when the sun went down the rapid tempo of the music fell.
"C'est la vie," say the old folks; it goes to show you never can tell.

They bought a souped-up jitney, 'twas a cherry-red fifty-nine,
They drove it down to New Orleans to celebrate their anniversary.
It was there where Pierre was wedded to the lovely mad'moiselle.
"C'est la vie," say the old folks; it goes to show you never can tell.

Uptown

He gets up each mornin' and he goes downtown,
Where ev'ryone's his boss and he's lost in any angry land;
He's a little man.
But then he comes uptown each evening to my tenement,
Uptown where folks don't have to pay much rent.
And when he's there with me, he can see that he's ev'rything.
Then he's tall, he don't crawl, he's a king.

Downtown he's just one of a million guys,
He don't get no breaks and he takes all they got to give,
'Cause he's gotta live.
But then he comes uptown where he can hold his head up high;
Uptown he knows that I'll be standin' by.
And when I take his hand, there's no man who could put him down.
The world is sweet, it's at his feet when he's uptown.

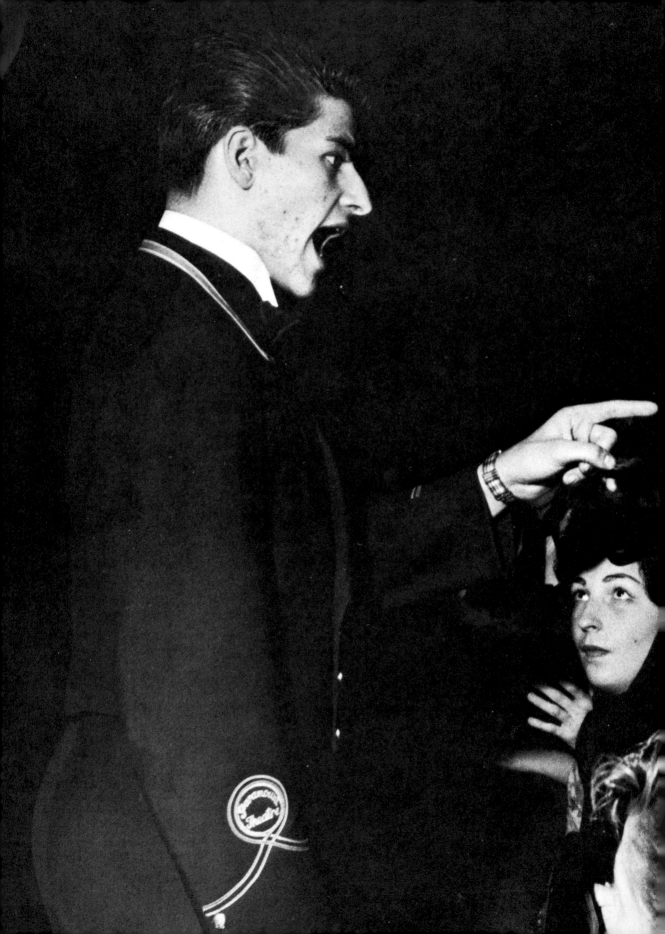

The Three Bells

There's a village hidden deep in the valley,
Among the pinetrees half forlorn,
And there on a sunny morning
Little Jimmy Brown was born.
So his parents brought him to the chapel,
When he was only one day old,
And the priest blessed the little fellow,
"Welcome, Jimmy, to the fold."

All the chapel bells were ringing
In the little valley town,
And the song that they were singing,
Was for baby Jimmy Brown.
Then the little congregation
Prayed for guidance from above,
"Lead us not into temptation,
Bless this hour of meditation,
Guide him with eternal love."

There's a village hidden deep in the valley,
Beneath the mountains high above,
And there, twenty years thereafter,
Jimmy was to meet his love.
Many friends were gathered in the chapel,
And many tears of joy were shed,
In June on a Sunday morning,
When Jimmy and his bride were wed.

All the chapel bells were ringing,
'Twas a great day in his life,
'Cause the song that they were singing
Was for Jimmy and his wife.
Then the little congregation
Prayed for guidance from above,
"Lead us not into temptation,
Bless, O Lord, this celebration,
May their lives be filled with love."

From the village hidden deep in the valley,
One rainy morning dark and gray,
A soul winged its way to heaven,
Jimmy Brown had passed away.
Silent people gathered in the chapel,
To say farewell to their old friend,
Whose life had been like a flower,
Budding blooming till the end.

Just a lonely bell was ringing
In the little valley town;
'Twas farewell that it was singing
To our good old Jimmy Brown.
And the little congregation
Prayed for guidance from above,
"Lead us not into temptation,
May his soul find the salvation
Of Thy great eternal love."

school

School Day
(Ring! Ring! Goes the Bell)

Up in the mornin' and out to school;
The teacher is teachin' the Golden Rule,
American hist'ry and practical math,
You study 'em hard and hopin' to pass.
Workin' your fingers right down to the bone,
An' the guy behind you won't leave you alone.

Ring! ring! goes the bell,
The cook in the lunchroom's ready to sell;
You're lucky if you can find a seat,
You're fortunate if you have time to eat.
Back in the classroom, open your books,
Gee, but the teacher don't know how mean she looks.

Soon as three o'clock rolls aroun',
You finally lay your burden down;
Close up your books, get outa your seat,
Down the hall an' into the street;
Up to the corner an' round the bend,
Right to the juke joint, you go in.

Drop the coin right into the slot,
You gotta hear somethin' that's really hot;
With the one you love you're makin' romance,
All day long you've been wantin' to dance.
Feelin' the music from head to toe,
'Round an' 'round an' 'round you go.

Hail! hail! rock 'n roll,
Deliver me from the days of old;
Long live rock ' roll,
The beat of the drums loud an' bold.
Rock! rock! rock 'n roll,
The feelin' is there, body an' soul.

Oh, Baby Doll

Oh, baby doll, when bells ring out the summer's free;
Oh, baby doll, will it end for you and me?
We'll sing the old alma mater and think of things that used to be.

I remember so well, back when the weather was cool;
We used to have so much fun when we were walkin' to school.
And if we stopped off to hear the latest songs they sing;
And we'd just make it in, before the bell would ring.

Oh, baby doll, when bells ring out the summer's free;
Oh, baby doll, will it end for you and me?
We'll sing the old alma mater and think of things that used to be.

When the teacher was gone, that's when we had a ball;
We used to dance and play all up and down the hall.
We had a portable radio, we was "ballin the jack";
But we'd all be back in order when the teacher got back.

Oh, baby doll, when bells ring out the summer's free;
Oh, baby doll, will it end for you and me?
We'll sing the old alma mater and think of things that used to be.

Be True to Your School

When some loud braggart tries to put me down and says his school is great,
I tell him right away now what's the matter buddy ain't you heard of my school — it's number
one in the state.

So be true to your school
Just like you would to your girl or guy;
Be true to your school now,
And let your colors fly;
Be true to your school.

I got a letterman's sweater with the letters in front I got from football and track;
I'm proud to wear it now when I cruise around the other parts of the town; I got my decal
in back.

So be true to your school
Just like you would to your girl or guy;
Be true to your school now,
And let your colors fly;
Be true to your school.

On Friday we'll be jacked up on the football game and I'll be ready to fight;
We're gonna smash 'em now, my girl will be workin' on her pompoms now, and she'll
be yellin' tonight.

So be true to your school
Just like you would to your girl or guy;
Be true to your school now,
And let your colors fly;
Be true to your school.

Graduation Day

It's a time for joy, a time for tears,
A time we'll treasure through the years.
We'll remember always
Graduation day.

At the senior prom we danced till three,
And then you gave your heart to me.
We'll remember always
Graduation day.

> Though we leave in sorrow
> All the joys we've known,
> We can face tomorrow
> Knowing we'll never walk alone.

When the ivy walls are far behind,
No matter where our path may wind,
We'll remember always
Graduation day.

wheels

Mabellene

Mabellene, why can't you be true?
Oh! Mabellene, why can't you be true?
You've started back doin' the things you used to do.

As I was motivatin' over the hill,
I saw Mabellene in a Coup de Ville;
A Cadillac a-rollin' on the ocean road,
Nothin' will outrun my v-eight Ford,
The Cadillac doin' 'bout ninety-five,
She's bumper to bumper, rollin' side by side.

Mabellene, why can't you be true?
Oh, Mabelleno, why can't you be true?
You've started back doin' the things you used to do

The Cadillac pulled up ahead of the Ford,
The Ford got hot and wouldn't do no more;
It then got cloudy and started to rain,
I tooted my horn for a passin' lane;
The rainwater blowin' all under my hood,
I know that I was doin' my motor good.

Mabellene, why can't you be true?
Oh, Mabellene, why can't you be true?
You've started back doin' the things you used to do.

The motor cooled down, the heat went down,
And that's when I heard that highway sound,
The Cadillac a-sittin' like a ton of lead,
A hundred and ten half a mile ahead,
The Cadillac lookin' like it's sittin' still
And I caught Mabellene at the top of the hill.

Mabellene, why can't you be true?
Oh! Mabellene, why can't you be true?
You've started back doin' the things you used to do.

Dead Man's Curve

I was cruisin' in my Stingray late one night,
When an XKE pulled up on the right.
He rolled down the window of his shiny new Jag
And challenged me then and there to a drag.
I said, "You're on, buddy, my mill's runnin' fine,
Let's come off the line now at Sunset and Vine.
But I'll go ya one better if ya got the nerve
Let's race all the way to Dead Man's Curve."
Dead Man's Curve,
Won't come back from Dead Man's Curve.

The street was deserted late Friday nite,
We were buggin' each other while we sat out the light.
We both popped the clutch when the light turned green;
You should have heard the whine from my screamin' machine.
I flew past La Brea, Schwabs and Crescent Heights,
And all the Jag could see were my six taillights.
He passed me at Doheny and I started to swerve,
But I pulled her out and there we were at Dead Man's Curve,
Dead Man's Curve.

> Well, the last thing I remember Doc, I started to swerve.
> And then I saw the Jag slide into the curb.
> I know I'll never forget that horrible sight
> And this I found out for myself, that everyone was right:

Won't come back from Dead Man's Curve,
Dead Man's Curve, Dead Man's Curve, Dead Man's Curve.
Ya won't come back from Dead Man's Curve, Dead
   Man's Curve, Dead Man's Curve, Dead Man's Curve.

(Seven Little Girls) Sitting in the Back Seat

Seven little girls sitting in the back seat
Huggin' and a-kissin' with Fred.
I said, "Why don't one of you come up and sit beside me?"
And this is what the seven girls said:

"All together now, one! two! three!
Keep your mind on your driving,
Keep your hands on the wheel,
Keep your snoopy eyes on the road ahead.
We're havin' fun sitting in the back seat
Kissin' and a-huggin' with Fred!"

Drove through the town, drove through the country,
Showed them how a motor could go.
I said, "How do you like my triple carburator?"
And one of 'em whispered low:

"All together now, one! two! three!
Keep your mind on your driving,
Keep your hands on the wheel,
Keep your snoopy eyes on the road ahead.
We're havin' fun sitting in the back seat
Kissin' and a-huggin' with Fred!"

Seven little girls smoochin' in the back seat,
Ev'ry one in love with Fred.
I said, "You don't need me, I'll get off at my house."
And this is what the seven girls said:

"All together now, one! two! three!
Keep your mind on your driving,
Keep your hands on the wheel,
Keep your snoopy eyes on the road ahead.
We're havin' fun sitting in the back seat
Kissin' and a-huggin' with Fred!"

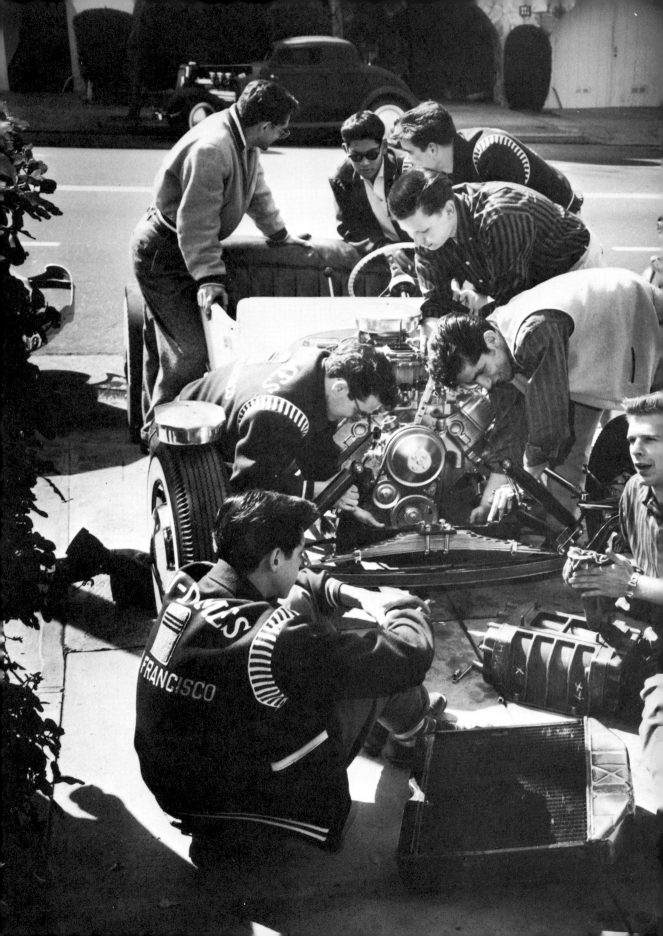

Car Trouble

Car trouble on a lonely road,
Car trouble on a lonely road.

I picked up my baby 'bout a quarter to eight,
Her dad said don't keep my girl out late —
Be back home 'bout a half past ten or else.

Car trouble on a lonely road,
Car trouble on a lonely road.

Didn't have time to go see a show —
Nothing to do, no place to go,
So we drove to the lake and we parked beneath the trees.

Car trouble on a lonely road,
Car trouble on a lonely road.

We were list'nin' to music on the radio,
Before we knew it, it was time to go.
I stepped on the starter and I didn't get a sound.

Car trouble on a lonely road,
Car trouble on a lonely road.

We started in walkin' back to town —
Couldn't get a ride, everybody turned us down.
As we walked in the gate I could hear her daddy yell.

Car trouble on a lonely road,
Car trouble on a lonely road.

So listen, you fellows, take a tip from me
Don't park too long beneath the trees,
'Cause if your car won't start your goose is cooked but good.

Little Deuce Coupe

Well I'm not braggin', babe, so don't put me down,
But I've got the fastest set of wheels in town.
When something pulls up to me it don't even try
And if it had a set of wings — man, I know I could fly.

She's my little deuce coupe —
You don't know what I got.

Just a little deuce coupe with a flat head mill
But she'll walk a Thunderbird like it's standin' still.
She's ported and relieved and she's stroked and bored,
She'll do a hundred and forty with the top end floored.

She's my little deuce coupe —
You don't know what I got.

She's got a competition clutch with four on the floor,
Yea, she purrs like a kitten 'till the lake pipes roar;
And if that ain't enough to make you flip your wig
There's one more thing — I got the pink slip daddy,
And comin' off the line when the light turns green
She blows 'em outta the water like you've never seen.
I get pushed out of shape and it's hard to steer
When I get rubber in all four gears.

She's my little deuce coupe —
You don't know what I've got.

Drag City

Burn up that quarter mile!
Just tuned my car now, she really peels,
A-lookin' real tough with chrome reversed wheels,
A Blue Coral wax job sure looks pretty,
Gonna get my chick and make it out to Drag City.

Yeah, I'm gonna Drag City, run her through now,
Gonna Drag City, what'll she do now?
Gonna Drag City, run her through now,
Gonna Drag City, what'll she do now?
Burn up that quarter mile!

The deejay is saying on my favorite station,
The Drag City races are the fastest in the nation.
Rails are the wildest and the stockers are pretty,
Gonna get my honey, grab some money, n' split to Drag City.

Yeah I'm gonna Drag City, run her through now,
Gonna Drag City, what'll she do now?
Gonna Drag City, run her through now,
Gonna Drag City, what'll she do now?
Burn up that quarter mile!

Burnin' rubber, thick exhaust fills the air,
Final tunes, tachin' up, action everywhere,
Checked flags, wheel stands, it sure sounds pretty,
To hear the cheers ring your ears, out at Drag City.

Yeah I'm gonna Drag City, run her through now,
Gonna Drag City, what'll she do now?
Gonna Drag City, run her through now,
Gonna Drag City, what'll she do now?
Burn up that quarter mile!

Shut Down

Tak it up, tak it up,
Buddy, gonna shut you down.

It happened on the strip where the road is wide,
Two cool shorts standin' side by side:
Yeah, my fuel-injected Stingray and a four-thirteen
Revin' up our engines and it sounds real mean.

Tak it up, tak it up,
Buddy, gonna shut you down.

Declinin' numbers at an even rate
At the count of one we both accelerate.
My Stingray is light, the slicks are startin' to spin
But the four-thirteen's wheels are diggin' in.

Gotta be cool, now,
Power shift, here we go.

The super-stock Dodge is windin' out in low,
But my fuel-injected Stingray's really startin' to go.
To get the traction I'm a ridin' the clutch,
My pressure plate's burnin', that machine's too much.
Pedal's to the floor, hear his dual-quad's drink,
And now the four-thirteen's lead is startin' to shrink.
He's hot with ram induction, but it's understood
I got a fuel-injected engine sittin' under my hood.

Shut it off, shut it off,
Buddy, now I shut you down.

The Little Old Lady (from Pasadena)

The little old lady from Pasadena
(Go, Granny, go, Granny, go, Granny, go)
Has a pretty little flower bed of white gardenias
(Go, Granny, go, Granny, go, Granny, go);
But parked in a rickety old garage
There's a brand-new shiny super-stocked Dodge.
And ev'rybody's sayin' that there's nobody meaner
Than the little old lady from Pasadena.

She drives real fast and she drives real hard,
She's the terror of Colorado Boulevard.
It's the little old lady from Pasadena!

If you see her on the strip, don't try to choose her
(Go, Granny, go, Granny, go, Granny, go),
You might have a goer, but you'll never lose her
(Go, Granny, go, Granny, go, Granny, go);
She's gonna get a ticket now, sooner or later,
'Cause she can't keep her foot off the accelerator.
And ev'rybody's sayin' that there's nobody meaner
Than the little old lady from Pasadena.

She drives real fast and she drives real hard,
She's the terror of Colorado Boulevard.
It's the little old lady from Pasadena!

You'll see her all the time, just gettin' her kicks now
(Go, Granny, go, Granny, go, Granny, go),
With her four-speed stick and a four-two-six now
(Go, Granny, go, Granny, go, Granny, go);
The guys come to race her from miles around,
But she'll give 'em a length, then she'll shut 'em down.
And ev'rybody's sayin' that there's nobody meaner
Than the little old lady from Pasadena.

She drives real fast and she drives real hard,
She's the terror of Colorado Boulevard.
It's the little old lady from Pasadena!

TEEN bEAT

Rock 'n Roll Music

Just let me hear some of that
Rock 'n roll music,
Any old way you choose it;
It's got a back beat, you can't lose it,
Any old time you use it.
It's gotta be rock-roll music,
If you wanna dance with me.
If you wanna dance with me.

I've got no kick against modern jazz,
Unless they try to play it too darn fast;
And change the beauty of the melody,
Until they sound just like a symphony.

That's why I go for that
Rock 'n roll music,
Any old way you choose it;
It's got a back beat, you can't lose it,
Any old time you use it.
It's gotta be rock-roll music,
If you wanna dance with me.
If you wanna dance with me.

I took my loved one over 'cross the tracks,
So she can hear my man awail a sax;
I must admit they have a rockin' band,
Man, they were goin' like a hurrican'.

That's why I go for that
Rock 'n roll music,
Any old way you choose it;
It's got a back beat, you can't lose it,
Any old time you use it.

It's gotta be rock-roll music,
If you wanna dance with me.
If you wanna dance with me.

'Way down South they gave a jubilee,
The jokey folks they had a jamboree;
They're drinkin' homebrew from a water cup,
The folks dancin' got all shook up

And started playin' that
Rock 'n roll music,
Any old way you choose it;
It's got a back beat, you can't lose it,
Any old time you use it.
It's gotta be rock-roll music,
If you wanna dance with me.
If you wanna dance with me.

Don't care to hear 'em play a tango,
I'm in the mood to hear a mambo;
It's 'way too early for a congo,
So keep a-rockin' that piano.

So I can hear some of that
Rock 'n roll music,
Any old way you choose it;
It's got a back beat, you can't lose it,
Any old time you use it.
It's gotta be rock-roll music,
If you wanna dance with me.
If you wanna dance with me.

Reelin' and Rockin'

Sometimes I will, then again I think I won't,
Sometimes I will, then again I think I won't,
Sometimes I do, then again I think I don't.

Well, I looked at my watch, it was nine-twenty-one,
'Twas at a rock 'n roll dance, havin' nothin' but fun;

We were rollin', reelin' and a-rockin';
We were reelin' and a-rockin' and rollin' till the break of dawn.

Well, I looked at my watch, it was nine-thirty-two,
There's nothin' I'd rather do, than dance with you;

We were rollin', reelin' and a-rockin';
We were reelin' and a-rockin' and rollin' till the break of dawn.

Well, I looked at my watch, it was nine-forty-three,
And every time I'd spin, she'd spin with me;

We were reelin', reelin' and a-rockin';
We were reelin' and a-rockin' and rollin' till the break of dawn.

Well, I looked at my watch, it was nine-fifty-four
I said, 'Dance, ballerina girl. Go! Go! Go!''

We were rollin', reelin' and a-rockin';
We were reelin' and a-rockin' and rollin' till the break of dawn.

Well, I looked at my watch, it was ten o' five,
Man, I didn't know whether I was dead or alive!

But I was rollin', reelin' and a-rockin';
We were reelin' and a-rockin' and rollin' till the break of dawn.

Well, I looked at my watch, it was ten-twenty-six,
But I'm a keep on dancin' till I got my kicks!

We were reelin', reelin' and a-rockin';
We were reelin' and a-rockin' and rollin' till the break of dawn.

Well, I looked at my watch, it was ten-twenty-eight,
I gotta get my kicks before it gets too late!

We were reelin', reelin' and a-rockin';
We were reelin' and a-rockin' and rollin' till the break of dawn.

Well, I looked at my watch, it was ten-twenty-nine,
I had to hold her hand, she was still holdin' mine!

We were reelin', reelin' and a-rockin';
We were reelin' and a-rockin' and rollin' till the break of dawn.

Well, I looked at my watch, and to my surprise,
I was dancin' with a woman that was twice my size!

We were reelin', reelin' and a-rockin';
We were reelin' and a-rockin' and rollin' till the break of dawn.

Well, I looked at my watch, and it was time to go,
The bandleader said, "We ain't playin' no mo'!"

We were reelin', reelin' and a-rockin';
We were reelin' and a-rockin' and rollin' till the break of dawn.

Mr. Bass Man

Mr. Bass Man, you got that certain something,
Mr. Bass Man, you set the music thumping.
To you it's easy when you go 1-2-3,
Baa, baa, ba ba ba,
You mean a ba ba ba ba ba ba.
Yea, Mr. Bass Man, you're on all the songs
With your dit dit dit ba ba ba ba;
Hey, Mr. Bass Man, you're head and king of rock 'n' roll,
Ba ba ba ba ba ba ba ba ba, no, no, no
Ba ba ba ba ba ba ba ba ba.
It don't mean a thing, when the leader's singing or when he goes
Ee yi ee yi ee yi yi.
Hey, Mr. Bass Man, I'll ask one question:
Will you teach me the way you sing?
Oh, Mr. Bass Man, I want to be a bass man too,
Ba ba ba ba ba ba ba ba, no no no
Ba ba ba ba ba ba ba ba ba.
Hey, Mr. Bass Man, I really think I'm with it,
With a ba ba ba ba ba ba ba ba
And a dit dit dit dit dit dit dit;
Oh come on, Mr. Bass Man, cause I'm a bass man too,
Ba, ba, ba, ba, ba, ba, ba, ba, ba, ba —
That's right, ba, ba, ba, ba, ba, ba, ba, ba . . .

Mr. Songwriter

I don't know any poetry;
How can I show what he means to me?

Oh, Mr. Songwriter, write me a song;
I want a song I can sing him,
A song that will bring him to me.

Make up some words that are all in rhyme
Words that will live till the end of time.

Oh, Mr. Songwriter, write me a song;
I want a song I can sing him,
A song that will bring him to me.

> A song like "Bless You,"
> Write me a song like "I Don't Wanna Cry";
> A song to tell him without him
> I just want to die.

Make up some words that are all in rhyme,
Words that will live till the end of time.

Oh, Mr. Songwriter, write me a song;
I want a song I can sing him,
A song that will bring him to me.

Around and Around

Say the joint was rockin',
Goin' 'round and 'round —
Yeah! Reelin' and rockin',
What a crazy sound.
Well they never stopped rockin'
Till the moon went down.

Oh, it sounds so sweet,
Gotta take me a chance;
Rose outa my seat,
Just had to dance.
Started movin' my feet.
Well, a-clappin' my hands.

Well, the joint started rockin',
Goin' 'round and 'round —
Yeah! Reelin' and rockin',
What a crazy sound.
Well they never stopped rockin'
Till the moon went down.

Twelve o'clock,
Well, the place was packed;
Front doors were locked,
Well the place was packed.
When the police knocked,
Both doors drew back.

But they kept on rockin',
Goin' 'round and 'round —
Yeah! Reelin' and rockin',
What a crazy sound.
Well they never stopped rockin'
Till the moon went down.

Papa Oom Mow Mow

Pa pa pa pa pa pa pa oom ma mow mow
Pa pa oom mow mow
Pa pa pa om-ma-ma ma mow
Pa pa oom mow mow
Oom a mow mow
Pa pa oom mow mow
Oo ma ma ma mow
Pa pa oom mow mow

Funniest sound I ever heard
Now I can't understand a single word.
Is he serious or is he playin'?
A oom mow mow is all he's say'n.

Pa pa oom oom mow mow
Pa pa oom mow mow
Pa pa pa oom mow mow
Pa pa oom mow mow
Pa pa pa oom mow mow
Pa pa oom mow mow
Pa pa pa oom mow mow

I said a-hey there, partner, what's your name?
Now don'tcha dare tell me the same old thing,
The words you're sayin' I can't figure out,
But you've gotta sound makes me stomp and shout!

Pa pa oom
Papa, papa, papa,
Hoo.

Now I hear this sound everywhere I go,
On the rock TV and radio;
And now it's spreading all over the land,
I still can't seem to understand.

Pa pa oom papa papa papa hoo . . .

Johnny B. Goode

Deep down in Lou'siana, close to New Orleans,
'Way back up in the woods among the evergreens;
There stood an old cabin made of earth and wood,
Where lived a country boy named Johnny B. Goode.
Who'd never ever learned to read or write so well,
But he could play a guitar just like a-ringin' bell.

Go! Go!
Go! Johnny! Go! Go!
Go! Johnny! Go! Go!
Go! Johnny! Go! Go!
Go! Johnny! Go! Go!
Johnny B. Goode.

He used to carry his guitar in a gunnysack,
Go sit beneath the tree by the railroad track;
Ol' engineer in the train sittin' in the shade,
Strummin' with the rhythm that the drivers made.
The people passin' by, they would stop and say,
Oh my, but that little country boy could play.

Go! Go!
Go! Johnny! Go! Go!
Go! Johnny! Go! Go!
Go! Johnny! Go! Go!
Go! Johnny! Go! Go!
Johnny B. Goode.

His mother told him, "Some day you will be a man
And you will be the leader of a big old band;
Many people comin' from miles around,
To hear you play your music till the sun goes down.
Maybe someday your name'll be in lights
A-sayin' 'Johnny B. Goode tonight.'"

Go! Go!
Go! Johnny! Go! Go!
Go! Johnny! Go! Go!
Go! Johnny! Go! Go!
Go! Johnny! Go! Go!
Johnny B. Goode.

Who Put the Bomp
(in the Bomp Ba Bomp Ba Bomp)

I'd like to thank the guy who wrote the song
That made my baby fall in love with me.

Who put the bomp in the bomp ba bomp ba bomp,
Who put the ram in the ram a lam a ding dong?
Who put the bop in the bop sh-bop sh-bop,
Who put the dit in the dit, dit, dit dit da?
Who was that man?
I'd like to shake his hand,
He made my baby fall in love with me.

When my baby heard
Bomp, ba ba bomp, ba bom ba bomp bomp,
Ev'ry word went right into her heart.
And when she heard them singing
Ram a lam a lam a lam a ding dong,
She said we'd never have to part.

Who put the bomp in the bomp ba bomp ba bomp,
Who put the ram in the ram a lam a ding dong?
Who put the bop in the bop sh-bop sh-bop,
Who put the dit in the dit, dit, dit dit da?
Who was that man?
I'd like to shake his hand,
He made my baby fall in love with me.

Time that we're alone —
Bomp, ba ba bomp, ba bom ba bomp bomp —
Sets my baby's heart all a-glow.
And ev'ry time we dance to
Ram a lam a lam a lam a ding dong,
She always says she loves me so.

Hully Gully, Baby

I went down to Miami
I met a girl named Sammy.
The moon was bright
The time was right;
I said, "Hey, girl, I love you —
What'ja wanna do?"

And she said.
"Hully gully, baby!
Hully gully, baby!
All! I! Wanna do with you
Is hully gully, baby!"

I spent my dough on Sammy
Hit every joint in Miami;
We danced all night
Till dawn's early bright.
I said, "Hey, girl, I love you —
Now what'ja wanna do?"

And she said,
"Hully gully, baby!
Hully gully, baby!
All! I! Wanna do with you
Is hully gully, baby!"

73

Splish Splash

Splish splash, I was takin' a bath
'Long about a Saturday night;
A-rub dub, just relaxin' in the tub,
Thinkin' ev'rything was all right.
Well, I stepped out the tub, put my feet on the floor;
I wrapped the towel around me and I opened the door.
And then a-splish splash,
I jumped back in the bath —
Well, how was I to know there was a party goin' on?

They was a-splishin' and a-splashin',
Reelin' with the feelin',
Rollin' and a-strollin',
Movin' and a-groovin', hey now!

I was a-splishin' and a-splashin',
I was a-rollin' and a-strollin',
I was a-movin' and a-groovin',
I was a-reelin' with the feelin',
I was a-rollin' and a-strollin', movin' and a-groovin',
Splish splash — yeah!

Bing bang, I saw the whole gang
Dancin' on my livin' room rug;
Flip flop, they were doin' the bop,
All the teens had the dancin' bug.
There was Lollipop with Peggy Sue,
Good golly, Miss Molly was-a even there too.
A-well-a splish splash,
I forgot about the bath,
I went and put my dancing shoes on.

I was a-rollin' and a-strollin',
Reelin' with the feelin',
Movin' and a-groovin',
Splishin' and a-splashin', hey now!

I was a-splishin' and a-splashin',
I was a-rollin' and a-strollin',
I was a-movin' and a-groovin',
I was a-reelin' with the feelin',
I was a-rollin' and a-strollin', movin' and a-groovin',
Splish splash — yeah!

75

Harry the Hairy Ape

Well, a strange thing happened the other night;
You won't believe it, but I swear it's true.
Harry, the hairy ape made his escape from the city zoo;
And under cover of darkness, he made his way to the middle of Municipal Park,
And hid in the bushes and waited for somebody to come walking along by hisself, in the dark.
Then, along come somebody, not suspecting nothing.
Harry jumped out of the bushes, all of a sudden . . .
Beat on his chest (thump, thump, thump) . . .
He jump up and down, and he say, "Hoo hoo hoo hoo hoo hoo hoo hoo hoo hoo hoo hoo hoo!"
Which is hairy-ape talk for "Boo! I betcha I scared you, ha ha!"
Wah! It scared that poor cat so bad, his eyes bugged out,
His hair turned white, and he run off through Municipal Park,
Screaming and hollering, tearing down the shrubbery, digging up the lawn,
Knocking down KEEP OFF THE GRASS signs, and run through the Hurricane fence,
And fell in the Municipal Swimming Pool and drowned hisself!!! Oh!

Well, Harry thought this were the funniest thing that-a he had ever seen.
And he laughed (ha-wheez-ha), jumped back in the bushes and got ready to do it again.
The next guy that come along was a near-sighted local deejay
Just bopping down the sidewalk on his way to work,
With a box of records under his arm that he was gonna play.
So here he come, not suspecting nothing;
Harry jumped out of the bushes all of a sudden,
Beat on his chest (thump, thump, thump),
Jumped up and down, and he say, "Hoo hoo hoo hoo hoo hoo hoo hoo hoo hoo hoo hoo
    hoo hoo!"
Which is hairy-ape talk for, "Boo! I betcha I scared you! Ha ha!"

Man, that radio announcer didn't even bat an eye.
He was so nearsighted, he thought Harry was a rock 'n' roll singer.
So he give him the old glad hand, slapped him on the back, smiled,
And say, "Don't worry man, I'm gonna play the record."
Then he say, "Bye!"
He bopped on off down the sidewalk, and every four or five steps
He'd stop and do a little "mashed potatoes."
Harry just stood there, watching till he got out of sight.
Man, he didn't know what to think.
I mean it really shook him up, and he run back to his cage,
Fast as he could go, and jumped up on his swing and put both hands over his eyes,
And didn't look for three hours and forty-five minutes.
But that's not the end of our story; no, here's what happened.

Well, the deejay played Harry's record. (What record? Shut up!)
It was a hit, and he became a star.
He got him some tight breeches, got him a manager,
Went on promotion tour, combed his hair back and took up playing guitar.
And every Sunday afternoon you can see Harry at the zoo,
And the girls'll scream and he'll sit on his swing,
And sing his hit record for you.
Hoo hoo hoo hoo — hooo hooo hooo — hoo hoo hoo hoo hooo hooo hooo —
Hoo hoo hoo hoo hoo hoo — hooo hooo hooo — .

loving feelings

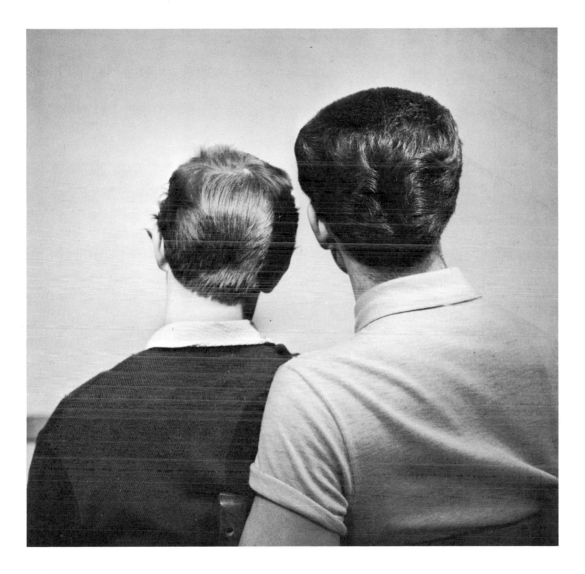

Pretty Woman

Hey, pretty woman walkin' down the street
You're the cutest thing I ever hope to meet;
Pretty woman,
Hey, hey, hey, pretty woman,
Now, there ain't nothin' in the world like a pretty, pretty girl,
Pretty woman.
You're a pretty woman in every way,
Lord, you're fine, well, hey, hey, hey;
But you need a lot of lovin', that's plain to see —
Hey, pretty woman, how about me?
Hey, pretty woman, are you headed my way?
Please, pretty woman, say yea, yea, yea,
Pretty woman,
Hey, hey, hey, pretty woman,
Now, there ain't nothin in the world like a pretty, pretty girl,
Pretty woman.

Come on baby, take me by the hand,
I'm gonna love you like no one can.
Pretty woman, you're somethin' to see
Pretty woman, you're O.K. by me.

Good Timin'

Oh you need timin',
A-tick-a, tick-a, tick-a good timin',
A-tock-a, tock-a, tock-a, tock-a — timin' is the thing,
It's true, good timin' brought me to you.

If little, little David hadn't grabbed that stone
A-lyin' there on the ground.
Big Goliath might've stomped on him
Instead of the other way around.

But he had timin'
A-tick-a, tick-a, tick-a good timin',
A-tock-a, tock-a, tock-a, tock-a — timin' is the thing,
It's true, good timin' brought me to you.

Who in the world would've ever known
What Columbus could do,
If Queen Izabella hadn't hocked her jewels
In fourteen-ninety-two?

But she had timin',
A-tick-a, tick-a, tick-a good timin',
A-tock-a, tock-a, tock-a, tock-a — timin' is the thing,
It's true, good timin' brought me to you.

What would've happened if you and I
Hadn't just happened to meet?
We might've spent the rest of our lives
Walkin' down Misery Street.

But we had timin',
A-tick-a, tick-a tick-a good timin'
A-tock-a, tock-a, tock-a, tock-a — timin' is the thing,
It's true, good timin' brought me to you.

Duke of Earl

As I walk through this world,
Nothing can stop the Duke of Earl,
And you are my girl,
And no one can hurt you.
Yes I'm gonna love you,
Let me hold you,
'Cause I'm the Duke of Earl.

When I hold you,
You will be the Duchess of Earl,
When I walk through my dukedom,
The paradise we will share.
I'm gonna love you,
Let me hold you,
'Cause I'm the Duke of Earl.

Silhouettes

Took a walk and passed your house late last night,
All the shades were pulled and drawn 'way down tight;
From within a dim light cast two silhouettes on the shade,
Oh what a lovely couple they made.
Put his arms around your waist, held you tight.
Kisses I could almost taste in the night,
Wondered why I'm not the guy
Whose silhouette's on the shade
I couldn't hide the tears in my eyes.
Ah . . .

Lost control and rang your bell; I was sore.
"Let me in, or else I'll beat down your door."
When two strangers who had been two silhouettes on the shade
Said to my shock, "You're on the wrong block."
Rushed down to your house with wings on my feet,
Loved you like I've never loved you, my sweet,
Vowed that you and I would be
Two silhouettes on the shade
All of our days, two silhouettes on the shade.
Ah . . .

Endless Sleep

The night was black, rain fallin' down;
Looked for my baby, she's nowhere aroun'.
Traced her footsteps down to the shore,
'Fraid she's gone for evermore.

I looked at the sea and it seemed to say,
"I took your baby from you away."
I heard a voice cryin' in the deep,
"Come join me, baby, in my endless sleep."

Why did we quarrel, why did we fight?
Why did I leave her alone tonight?
That's why her footsteps ran into the sea,
That's why my baby has gone from me.

I looked at the sea and it seemed to say,
"I took your baby from you away."
I heard a voice cryin' in the deep,
"Come join me, baby, in my endless sleep."

Ran in the water, heart full of fear;
There in the breakers I saw her near.
Reached for my darlin', held her to me,
Stole her from the angry sea.

I looked at the sea and it seemed to say,
"You took your baby from me away."
My heart cried out, "She's mine to keep!"
I saved my baby from an endless sleep.

Aladdin

I had a strange, exciting dream last night;
I was a wanderer with no love in sight,
When all at once I saw his magic light.
Aladdin — standing there.

He asked me if I had a wish to make,
I thought of you and knew the wish I'd take;
He rubbed his lamp and then he set away.
Aladdin — I'm on my way.

I've come to tell you of my love;
He said that you care, too.
Now in your arms I know he's right;
He made it all come true.

I'd like to meet him in a dream tonight
And give our thanks for showing me the light;
I'd like to tell him he was oh so right.
Aladdin — now she's mine.

Aladdin — Aladdin — Aladdin.

The Boy from New York City

Oo-wah oo-wah cool, cool Kitty,
Tells us about the boy from New York City.
Oo-wah oo-wah, come on, Kitty,
Tell us about the boy from New York City.

He's kinda tall; he's really fine.
Some day I hope to make him mine, all mine.
And he's neat and oh so sweet,
And just the way he looked at me swept me off my feet.
Ooh ee, you ought to come and see
How he walks,
And how he talks.

Ev'ry time he says he loves me,
Chills run down my spine.
Ev'ry time he wants to kiss me
Ooh, he makes me feel so fine — yeah!

Oo-wah oo-wah, come on, Kitty,
Tell us about the boy from New York City.
Oo-wah oo-wah, come on, Kitty,
Tell us about the boy from New York City.

He's really down, and he's no clown.
He has the finest penthouse I've ever seen in town.
And he's cute in his mohair suit,
And he keeps his pockets full of spending loot.
Ooh ee, you ought to come and see
His pretty bar,
And his brand-new car.

Ev'ry time he says he loves me,
Chills run down my spine.
Ev'ry time he wants to kiss me,
Ooh, he makes me feel so fine — yeah!

Oo-wah, oo-wah, come on, Kitty,
Tell us about the boy from New York City.
Oo-wah, oo-wah, come on, Kitty,
Tell us about the boy from New York City.

He can dance and make romance,
And that's when I fell in love with just one glance.
He was shy, and so was I.
And now I know we'll never ever say good-bye.
Ooh ee, you ought to come and see.
He's the most
From coast to coast.

Ev'ry time he says he loves me,
Chills run down my spine.
Ev'ry time he wants to kiss me,
Ooh, he makes me feel so fine, yeah!

Oo-wah, oo-wah, come on, Kitty,
Tells us about the boy from New York City.
Oo-wah, oo-wah, come on, Kitty,
Tell us about the boy from New York City.

Who Do You Love?

I walk forty-seven miles of barb wire,
I use a cobra snake for a necktie,
I got a brand-new house on the roadside
Made from rattlesnake hide,
I got a brand-new chimney made up on top
Made out of a human skull.
Now come on take a walk with me, Arlene
And tell me
Who do you love?
Who do you love?

Tombstone hand and graveyard mind
I'm just twenty-two and I don't mind dying.
Who do you love?

I go out on the town, use a rattlesnake whip
Take it easy, Arlene, don't give me no lip.
Who do you love?

The night was dark, the sky was blue,
Down the alley an ice wagon flew
Hit a bump and somebody screamed
You should have heard just what I seen.
Who do you love?

Arlene took me by my hand,
She said, "Oowee bo, you know I understand."
Who do you love?
Who do you love?

Norman

Jimmy called me on the phone,
But I was gone, not at home,
'Cause I was out parked all alone
With darlin' Norman.

Norman holds me close to him,
Norman kisses me, and then
Norman knows my heart belongs to him, and him, and only him, oh.

Norman,
Oooo, Norman,
Oooo, Norman,
Norman my love.

Bill invited me to a show,
But I said, "no, cannot go —
There's a dress that I've got to sew
And wear for Norman."

Norman is my only love,
Norman's all I'm thinking of;
Norman gives me all his lovin', kissin', huggin', lovey dovin'.

Norman,
Oooo Norman,
Oooo Norman,
Norman my love.

Joey asked me for a date,
He wanted to take me out to skate;
But I told Joey he would have to make
Arrangements with Norman.

Norman is my only love
Norman's all I'm thinking of
Norman gives me all his lovin', kissin', huggin', lovey dovin'.

Norman,
Oooo, Norman,
Oooo, Norman,
Norman my love.

She Was Only Seventeen
(He Was One Year More)

She was only seventeen, he was one year more;
She loved him with all her heart and he the girl adored.
But our friends believed they were too young to know the score,
'Cause she was only seventeen, he was one year more.

Are they old enough to know if love will last for life?
Isn't he too young to be a husband, her a wife?
Well, in the past I'll bet it's happened more than once before
When someone else was seventeen, another one year more.

Do we have the right to question love that seems so strong?
As long as God has no objection, there can be no wrong.
Let us be the first to wish them all the very best,
Let us hope their love is strong enough to meet the test.
'Cause like I say, I'll bet it's happened more than once before
When someone else was seventeen, another one year more.

Judy's Turn to Cry

When Judy left with Johnny at my party,
And came back wearing his ring,
I sat down and cried my eyes out;
Now that was a foolish thing.

'Cause now it's Judy's turn to cry,
Judy's turn to cry,
Judy's turn to cry,
'Cause Johnny's come back to me.

It hurt me so to see them dance together
I felt like making a scene;
Then my tears just fell like raindrops,
'Cause Judy's smile was so mean.

But now it's Judy's turn to cry,
Judy's turn to cry,
Judy's turn to cry,
'Cause Johnny's come back to me.

One night I saw them kissing at a party,
So I kissed some other guy.
Johnny jumped up and hit him,
'Cause he still loved me, that's why.

So now it's Judy's turn to cry,
Judy's turn to cry,
Judy's turn to cry,
'Cause Johnny's come back to me.

Teen-age Sonata

Oh ah, oh ah, oh ah, oh ah, mm.

Here, here in the moonlight,
Hold me while I sing to you;
My teen-age sonata,
Of my love eternally true.
It's written and filled with devotion
From deep in my heart;
And with my teen-age sonata,
Comes a pray'r that we'll never part.
And as long as we love it will stay,
Oh, we'll hear it on our wedding day.
Oh ah, oh ah, oh ah, oh ah.

My, my lips can only kiss you,
They can't explain how you make me feel.
But my teen-age sonata
Will tell you that my love is real.
My love is real, oh ah,
My, my, my, my, my love is real.
Oh ah, oh ah,
Oh ah, oh ah.

HEARTBREAK

Donna

I had a girl, Donna was her name;
Since she left me, I've never been the same,
'Cause I love my girl.
Donna, where can you be?
Where can you be?

Now that you're gone, I'm left all alone,
All by myself to wander and roam.
How I love my girl!
Donna, where can you be?
Where can you be?

> Well, Donna, now that you're gone,
> I don't know what I'll do.
> All the time and all my love for you, just for you!

I had a girl, Donna was her name;
Since she's been gone, I've never been the same,
'Cause I love my girl.
Donna, where can you be?
Where can you be?

A White Sport Coat
(and a Pink Carnation)

A white sport coat and a pink carnation —
I'm all dressed up for the dance.
A white sport coat and a pink carnation —
I'm all alone in romance.

> Once you told me long ago
> To the prom with me you'd go.
> Now you've changed your mind it seems;
> Someone else will hold my dreams.

A white sport coat and a pink carnation —
I'm in a blue, blue mood.

Come On

Ev'rything is wrong since me and my baby parted,
All day long I'm walkin' 'cause I couldn't get my car started;
Laid off from my job and I can't afford to check it,
I wish somebody'd come along and run into it and wreck it.

Come on,
Since my baby parted, come on,
I can't get started, come on,
I can't afford to check it,
I wish somebody'd come along and run into it and wreck it.

Ev'rything is wrong since I've been without you,
Ev'ry night I lie awake thinkin' about you;
Ev'rytime the phone rings sounds like thunder —
Some stupid jerk tryin' to reach another number.

Come on,
Since I've been without you, come on,
Steady thinkin' bout you, come on,
Phone sounds like thunder,
There's some stupid jerk tryin' to reach another number.

Ev'rything is wrong since I last saw you, baby;
I really want to see you and I don't mean maybe.
I'm doin' everything tryin' to make you see
That I belong to you, honey, and you belong to me.

So come on,
I wanna see you baby, come on,
I don't mean maybe, come on,
I'm trying' to make you see
That I belong to you and you belong to me.

Mr. Blue

I'm Mr. Blue
When you say you love me,
Then prove it by goin' out on the sly,
Provin' your love isn't true —
Call me Mr. Blue.

I'm Mr. Blue,
When you say you're sorry,
Then turn around, headin' for the lights of town,
Hurtin' me thru and thru —
Call me Mr. Blue.

> I stay at home at night,
> Right by the phone at night,
> But you won't call and I won't hurt my pride —
> Call me Mr.

I won't tell you
While you paint the town
A bright red to turn it upside down,
I'm painting it too,
But I'm painting it blue.
Call me Mr. Blue.

Fortune Teller

Fortune teller, can you see
What my future's going to be?
Can you see it all in your crystal ball,
Have you got a dream for me?

Fortune teller, is she free
Has she waited just for me?
You can see it all in your crystal ball;
Tell me that it's meant to be.

Tell me, tell me, tell me.

Will we meet on a busy corner,
Will she know that I'm the one?
Will I be like Little Jack Horner,
Get myself a sugar plum?

Fortune teller, will she stay
Close beside me all the way?
You have seen it all in your crystal ball;
She's the only love for me.

Fortune teller, is she free
Has she waited just for me?
You can see it all in your crystal ball;
Tell me that it's meant to be.

Tell me, tell me, tell me.

Will we meet on a busy corner,
Will she know that I'm the one?
Will I be like Little Jack Horner,
Get myself a sugar plum?

Fortune teller, will she stay
Close beside me all the way?
You have seen it all in your crystal ball;
Gotta find the dream you see.

Whoa, whoa, she's the only love for me,
She's the only love for me.

Crying

I was all right for a while
I could smile for a while;
But I saw you last night,
You held my hand real tight
As you stopped to say hello.
Oh, you wished me well,
You couldn't tell
That I'd been crying over you
Crying over you.
When you said so long,
Left me standing all alone
Alone and crying, crying, crying, crying,
It's hard to understand,
But the touch of your hand
Can start me crying.

I thought that I was over you,
But it's true, so true
I love you even more
Than I did before.
But darling, what can I do?
For you don't love me
And I'll always be
Crying over you,
Crying over you.
Yes, now you're gone
And from this moment on
I'll be crying, crying, crying, crying,
Yeah, crying, crying over you.

Breaking Up Is Hard to Do

Don't take your love away from me,
Don't you leave my heart in misery,
Yet you know that I'll be blue,
'Cause breaking up is hard to do.
Remember when you held me tight
And you kissed me all through the night?
Think of all that we've been through
And breaking up is hard to do.

    They say that breaking up is hard to do,
    And I know that I know that it's true;
    Don't say that this is the end,
    Instead of breaking up I wish that we were making up again.

I beg of you, don't say good-bye.
Can't we give our love another try?
Come on, baby, let's start anew,
'Cause breaking up is hard to do.

Thirty Days (to Come Back Home)

I'm gonna give you thirty days to get back home,
I'm gonna call up the gypsy woman on the telephone.
I'm gonna send out a world-wide hoo-doo,
That'll be the very thing that'll suit you —
I'm gonna see that you'll be back home in thirty days.

Oh, thirty days,
Oh, thirty days,
Baby, I'll see that you'll be back home in thirty days.
Well, I'm gonna send out a world-wide hoo-doo,
That'll be the very thing that'll suit you,
I'm gonna see that you'll be back home in thirty days.

I've talked to the judge in private early this morning,
I'm goin' to the sheriff's office to sign a warrant.
I'm gonna put across a charge agin' ya,
That'll be the very thing that'll send ya —
I'm gonna see that you'll be back home in thirty days.

Oh, thirty days,
Oh, thirty days,
Baby, I'll see that you'll be back home in thirty days.
Well, I'm gonna put across a charge agin' ya,
That'll be the very thing that'll send ya,
I'm gonna see that you'll be back home in thirty days.

If I don't get no satisfaction from the judge,
I'm gonna take it to the FBI as a personal grudge.
If they don't give me no consolation,
I'm gonna take it to the United Nations.
I'm gonna see that you'll be back home in thirty days.

Oh, thirty days,
Oh, thirty days,
Baby, I'll see that you'll be back home in thirty days.
Well, if they don't give me no consolation,
I'm gonna take it to the United Nations,
I'm gonna see that you'll be back home in thirty days.

Torture

Torture, torture,
Baby, you're torturing me.

Why do you lead me around and make me chase ya?
When I catch ya, you won't let me embrace ya.
Please baby, have a heart 'cause can't you see
You're torturing me,
Torturing me.

This torture that I'm going through
Is worth the pain if I have you.
So if you love me, let me know;
But if you don't, please let me go.
Torture, torture,
Baby, you're torturing me.

You know that I'm crazy about you,
Yet you make me do without you.
Do you mean to hurt or don't you see
You're torturing me,
Torturing me.

TRAGEDY

Ebony Eyes

On a weekend pass I wouldn't have had time
To get home and marry that Baby of mine.
So I went to the chaplain and he authorized
Me to send for my ebony eyes.

My ebony eyes was coming to me
From out of the skies on flight twelve o three,
In an hour or two I would whisper "I do"
To my beautiful ebony eyes.

The plane was way overdue so I went inside to the airlines desk,
And I said, "Sir, I wonder why flight twelve-o-three is so late?"
He said, "Oh they probably took off late,
Or they may have run into turbulent weather
And had to alter their course."
I went back outside and I waited at the gate
And watched the beacon light from the control tower
As it whipped through the dark ebony skies
As if it were searching for my ebony eyes.
Then came the announcement over the loud speaker,
"Would those having relatives or friend on flight number twelve-o-three
Please report to the chapel across the street at once."

Then I felt a burning break deep inside,
And I knew the heavenly ebony skies
Had taken my life's most wonderful prize,
My beautiful ebony eyes.

If I ever get to heaven I'll bet
My first angel I'll recognize.
She'll smile at me and I know she will be
My beautiful ebony eyes.

Teen Angel

That fateful night the car was stalled upon the railroad track,
I pulled you out and we were safe but you went running back.

Teen angel, can you hear me; Teen angel, can you see me?
Are you somewhere up above, And am I still your own true love?

What was it you were looking for that took your life that night?
They said they found my high school ring clutched in your fingers tight.

Teen angel, can you hear me; Teen angel, can you see me?
Are you somewhere up above, And am I still your own true love?

Just sweet sixteen and now you're gone, they've taken you away;
I'll never kiss your lips again, they buried you today.

Teen angel, can you hear me; Teen angel, can you see me?
Are you somewhere up above, And am I still your own true love?

Last Kiss

Well oh where, oh where can my baby be?
The Lord took her away from me.
She's gone to heaven so I got to be good
So I can see my baby when I leave this world.

We were out on a date in my daddy's car,
We hadn't driven very far,
When there in the road straight ahead
A car was stalled, the engine was dead.
I couldn't stop, so I swerved to the right
I'll never forget the sound that night
The crying tires, the busting glass
The painful screams that I heard last.

Well oh where, oh where can my baby be?
The Lord took her away from me.
She's gone to heaven so I got to be good
So I can see my baby when I leave this world.

Well when I woke up the rain was pouring down;
There was people standing all around.
Something warm running in my eyes
But I found my baby somehow that night.
I raised her head, then she smiled and said,
"Hold me, darling, for a little while."
I held her close, I kissed her, our last kiss,
I found her love that I knew I'd miss.

But now she's gone, even though I hold her tight
I lost my love — my life — that night.

Well oh where, oh where can my baby be?
The Lord took her away from me.
She's gone to heaven so I got to be good
So I can see my baby when I leave this world.

Tell Laura I Love Her

Laura and Tommy were lovers,
He wanted to give her ev'rything,
Flowers, presents, and most of all a wedding ring!
He saw a sign for a stock-car race,
A thousand-dollar prize it read;
He couldn't get Laura on the phone,
So to her mother Tommy said:

"Tell Laura I love her! Tell Laura I need her!
Tell Laura I may be late; I've something to do that cannot wait."

He drove his car to the racing grounds,
He was the youngest driver there;
The crowd roared as they started the race,
'Round the track they drove at a deadly pace!
No one knows what happened that day,
How his car overturned in flames,
But as they pulled him from the twisted wreck,
With his dying breath, they heard him say:

"Tell Laura I love her! Tell Laura I need her!
Tell Laura not to cry; my love for her will never die!"

Now in the chapel Laura prays
For her Tommy who passed away;
It was just for Laura he lived and died,
Alone in the chapel she can hear him cry;

"Tell Laura I love her! Tell Laura I need her!
Tell Laura not to cry; my love for her will never die!"

Running Bear

On the bank of the river stood Running Bear, young Indian brave.
On the other side of the river stood his lovely Indian maid.
Little White Dove was her name, such a lovely sight to see.
But their tribes fought with each other, so their love could never be.

Running Bear loved Little White Dove
With a love big as the sky.
Running Bear loved Little White Dove
With a love that couldn't die.

He couldn't swim the raging river 'cause the river was too wide.
He couldn't reach Little White Dove waiting on the other side.
In the moonlight he could see her, throwing kisses across the waves.
Her little heart was beating faster, waiting there for her brave.

Running Bear loved Little White Dove
With a love big as the sky.
Running Bear loved Little White Dove
With a love that couldn't die.

Running Bear dove in the water, Little White Dove did the same;
And they swam out to each other — through the swirling stream they came.
As their hands touched and their lips met the raging river pulled them down.
Now they'll always be together in that Happy Hunting Ground.

Running Bear loved Little White Dove
With a love big as the sky.
Running Bear loved Little White Dove
With a love that couldn't die.

Moody River

Moody River, more deadly than the vainest knife;
Moody River, your muddy water took my baby's life.

Last Saturday evening I came to the old oak tree
That stands beside the river where you were to meet me.
On the ground your glove I found with a note addressed to me.
It read, "Dear love, I've done you wrong. Now I must set you free.
No longer can I live with this hurt and this sin.
I just couldn't tell you that guy was just a friend."

Moody River, more deadly than the vainest knife;
Moody River, your muddy water took my baby's life.

I looked into the muddy water and what could I see?
I saw a lonely, lonely face just lookin' back at me;
Tears in his eyes and a prayer on his lips
And the glove of his lost love at his fingertips.

Moody River, more deadly than the vainest knife;
Moody River, your muddy water took my baby's life.

Patches

Down by the river that flows by the coalyards
Stand wooden houses with shutters torn down.
There lives a girl ev'rybody calls Patches,
Patches, my darling of old Shanty Town.

We planned to marry when June brought the sun;
I couldn't wait to make Patches my bride.
Now I don't see how that ever can happen;
My folks say no and my heart breaks inside.

Patches, oh what can I do?
I swear I'll always love you.
But a girl from that place will just bring me disgrace,
So my folks won't let me love you.

Each night I cry as I think of that shanty
And pretty Patches there watching the door.
She doesn't know that I can't come to see her.
Patches must think I love her no more.

I hear a neighbor telling my father
He says a girl name of Patches was found
Floating face down in that dirty old river
That flows by the coalyards in old Shanty Town.

Patches, oh what can I do?
I swear I'll always love you.
It may not be right but I'll join you tonight.
Patches, I'm coming to you.

HARD TIMES

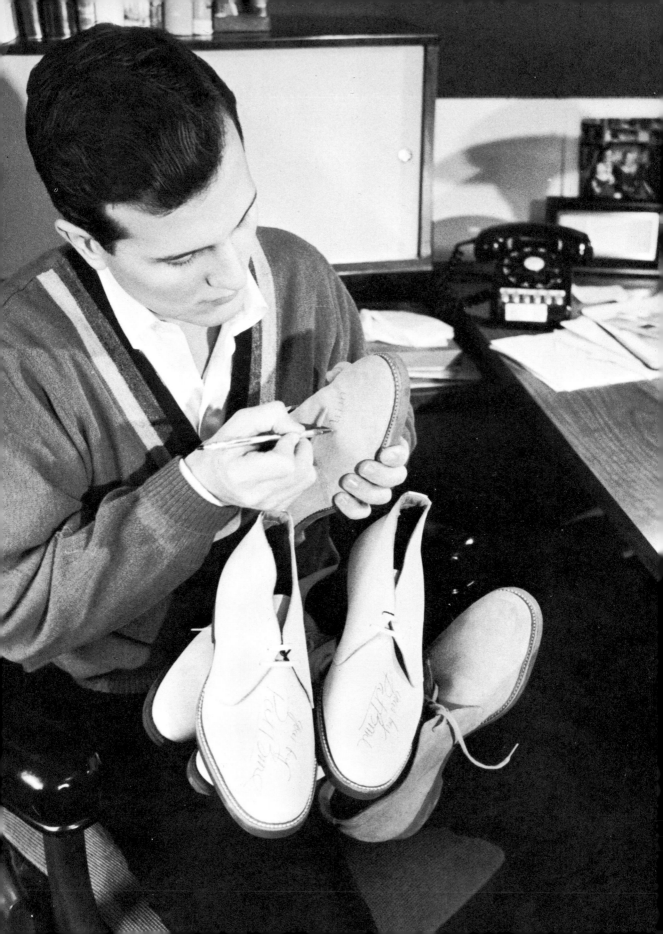

Get a Job

Sha da da da
Sha da da da da
Sha da da da
Sha da da da da
Sha da da da
Sha da da da da
Sha da da da
Sha da da da da
Yip yip yip yip
Yip yip yip yip
Mum mum mum mum
Mum mum
Get a job.
Sha da da da
Sha da da da da.

Every mornin' about this time
She get me out of my bed
A-crying "Get a job."
After breakfast, every day,
She throws the want ads right my way
And never fails to say
"Get a job."

Sha da da da
Sha da da da da
Sha da da da
Sha da da da da
Sha da da da
Sha da da da da
Sha da da da
Sha da da da da
Yip yip yip yip
Yip yip yip yip
Mum mum mum mum
Mum mum

Get a job.
Sha da da da
Sha da da da da.

And when I get the paper
I read it through and through
And my girl never fails to see
If there is any work for me.
And when I go back to the house
I hear the woman's mouth
Preaching and a-crying,
Tell me that I'm lying 'bout a job,
That I never could find.

Sha da da da
Sha da da da da
Sha da da da
Sha da da da da
Sha da da da
Sha da da da da
Sha da da da
Sha da da da da
Yip yip yip yip
Yip yip yip yip
Mum mum mum mum
Mum mum
Get a job.
Sha da da da
Sha da da da da
Uh-huh
Sha da da da
Sha da da da da
Uh-huh . . .

Blue Monday

Blue Monday, how I hate blue Monday,
Have to work like a slave all day.
Here comes Tuesday, oh hard Tuesday,
I'm so tired I've got no time to play.
Here comes Wednesday, I'm beat to my socks,
My gal calls, got to tell her that I'm out,
Cause Thursday is a hard working day,
And Friday I get my pay.

Saturday morning, oh Saturday morning,
All my tiredness has gone away.
Got my money, and my honey
And I'm out on the stem to play.

Sunday morning my head is bad,
But it's worth it for the time I have had.
But I got to get my rest,
Cause Monday is next.

Money Honey

The landlord rang my front door bell,
I let him ring for a long long spell;
I went to the window and peeped through the blind
And asked him to tell me what was on his mind
He said

"Money honey, (yeah------)
Money honey, (mmm------)
Money honey,
If you wanna stay here with me!"

I was clean as a screen and so hard pressed
So I called the one that I love best;
I fin'lly got my baby 'bout half past three.
She said, "I'd like to know what you want with me!"
I said,

"Money honey, (yeah------)
Money honey, (mmm------)
Money honey,
If you wanna get along with me!"

She screamed and said, "What's wrong with you?
From this day on our romance is through!"
I said, "Tell me, baby, face to face,
How could another man take my place?"
She said,

"Money honey, (yeah--------)
Money honey, (mmm--------)
Money honey,
If you wanna get along with me!"

Now I've learned my lesson and now I know
The sun may shine and the winds may blow,
Women may come and women may go,
But before I'll say I love 'em so
I want

Money honey, (yeah--------)
Money honey, (mmm--------)
Money honey,
If you wanna get along with me!

Let It Rock

In the heat of the day down in Mobile, Alabama,
Workin' on the railroad with a steel-drivin' hammer;
I gotta get some money and buy some brand-new shoes,
Try to find somebody to take away these blues.
She don't love me, hear 'em singin' in the sun,
Payday comin' when my work is all done.

Well, in the evenin' when the sun is sinkin' low,
All the ovens waitin' for the whistles to blow;
A-sittin' in the teepee built right on the track,
Rollin' them bones till the foreman comes back,
Pick up your belongings, boys, scatter about
We got all schedule train comin' two miles out.

Ev'rybody's scramblin' and jumpin' around,
Pickin' up the money, tearin' the teepee down;
Our foreman was a panic, 'bout to go insane,
Tryin' to get the workers out of the way of the train.
Engineer blowin' the whistle long and long,
Can't stop the train, he has to let it roll on.

Busted

My bills are all due and the baby needs shoes and I'm busted.
Cotton is down to a quarter a pound, but I'm busted.
I got a cow that went dry and a hen that won't lay
And a big stack of bills that gets bigger each day
The county's gonna haul my belongings away, 'cause I'm busted.

I went to my brother to ask for a loan, 'cause I was busted.
I hate to beg like a dog without his bone, but I'm busted.
My brother said, "There ain't a thing I can do,
My wife and kids are all down with the flu;
And I was just thinking of calling on you, and I'm busted."

Well, I am no thief but a man can go wrong, when he's busted.
The food that we canned all last summer is gone, and I'm busted.
The fields are all bare and the cotton won't grow,
Me and my family got to pack up and go,
But I'll make a living, just where I don't know,
'Cause I'm busted.
I'm broke . . . no bread . . .
I mean like nothin' . . . forget it.

Leroy

I know a boy, he was never blue,
Now he lives in cell block two;
I don't know just why he's blue;
Leroy! What did you do?

Oh! Leroy's back in jail again!
Leroy's back in jail again;
I don't know why, why he's blue,
Leroy! What did you do?

I went to the judge, said, "Dig man, wail!
I'm here and I gotta Leroy's bail!"
The judge said, "Son, don't you tell me no tale,
Leroy, he's gonna stay in jail!"

Oh! Leroy's back in jail again!
Leroy's back in jail again;
I don't know why, why he's blue,
Leroy! What did you do?

Now Leroy said, "Man, you tried your best!
Now I'm here, I'm gonna take a rest!
Now see Minnie, she's got the blues;
She'll let you wear my long pointed shoes!"

Oh! Leroy's back in jail again!
Leroy's back in jail again;
I don't know why, why he's blue,
Leroy! What did you do?

Leroy's heart is full of hate;
Leroy, he just can't go straight;
"Tell my Minnie, can't keep my date;
I'm gonna be 'bout six months late!"

Oh! Leroy's back in jail again!
Leroy's back in jail again;
I don't know why, why he's blue,
Leroy! What did you do?
Leroy! What did you do?

Stagger Lee

I was standing on the corner when I heard my bulldog bark,
He was barking at the two men who were gambling in the dark.
It was Stagger Lee and Billy, two men who gamble late,
Stagger Lee threw seven, Billy swore that he threw eight.

Stagger Lee told Billy, "I can't let you go with that,
You have won all my money and my brand-new Stetson hat."
Stagger Lee went home, and he pulled his forty-four,
Said, "I'm going to the barroom just to pay that debt I owe."

Stagger Lee went to the barroom, and he stood across the barroom door,
Said, "Now nobody move" and he pulled his forty-four.
"Stagger Lee," cried Billy, "Oh, please don't take my life.
I got three little children, and a very sickly wife."
Stagger Lee shot Billy, oh, he shot that poor boy so bad,
Till the bullet came through Billy, and it broke the bartender's glass.

Look out now,
    Go, go Stagger Lee.
    Go, go Stagger Lee.
    Go, go Stagger Lee.
    Go, go Stagger Lee.
    Go, go Stagger Lee.
    Go, go Stagger Lee.
    Go, go Stagger Lee.
    Go, go!

Heartbreak Hotel

Now since my baby left me
I've found a new place to dwell,
Down at the end of Lonely Street
At Heartbreak Hotel.

I'm so lonely,
I'm so lonely,
I'm so lonely,
That I could die.

And tho' it's always crowded,
You can still find some room
For broken-hearted lovers
To cry there in the gloom

And be so lonely,
Oh, so lonely,
Oh, so lonely,
They could die.

The bellhop's tears keep flowing,
The desk clerk's dressed in black.
They've been so long on Lonely Street,
They never will go back.

And they're so lonely,
Oh, they're so lonely,
They're so lonely
They pray to die.

So if your baby leaves
And you have a tale to tell,
Just take a walk down Lonely Street
To Heartbreak Hotel,

Where you'll be so lonely,
And I'll be so lonely,
We'll be so lonely
That we could die.

PICTURE CREDITS

index of songs
and their composers